Christmas in Auschwitz

Christmas in Auschwitz
András Mezei
Translated and edited by Thomas Ország-Land

Published 2010 by
Smokestack Books
PO Box 408, Middlesbrough TS5 6WA
e-mail : info@smokestack-books.co.uk
www.smokestack-books.co.uk

Christmas in Auschwitz
András Mezei
Original text copyright by the heirs of András Mezei.
English translation copyright 2010 by Thomas Ország-Land.
Cover image: courtesy Krisztián Ungváry
Photo of András Mezei: courtesy Gábor Mezei

Printed by
EPW Print & Design Ltd

ISBN 978-0-9560341-9-9
Smokestack Books gratefully
acknowledges the support of
Arts Council England

Smokestack Books is
represented by Inpress Ltd
www.inpressbooks.co.uk

Contents

- 9 András Mezei, Poetry and the Holocaust
- 14 Faces
- 15 Flames
- 16 Blue Eyes
- 17 Friday Evening
- 19 Voices
- 20 The Lists
- 21 Poor Folk
- 22 Robbery, Naked
- 23 Memorandum
- 24 Letter from Nusi
- 25 Deportation
- 26 The Roma
- 27 Haste
- 28 Deported Women
- 29 A Chorus of Pious Souls
- 30 A Choice
- 31 Hiding
- 32 Tumbrils
- 33 Roma Campsite
- 34 A Camp by the Village
- 35 Statistics
- 36 Delight
- 37 His Own Command
- 38 Jason
- 39 Gustav!
- 40 Testimony
- 41 Psalm
- 42 Before my Fall
- 43 The Masters
- 44 In the Bomb-Pit
- 45 Tally
- 46 My Folk
- 47 Towards the Dniester

48 Cattle-Trucks
49 Possessions
50 The Executioners
51 Self-Portrait, Treblinka
52 Christmas in Auschwitz
53 The Scale
54 Group Portrait
55 Hunger: Data
56 If the Mother...
57 In their Place: A Daughter
58 Exhumation
59 Nightmares: The Survivor
60 The Street of the Dead
61 Blanche Schwarcz
62 I Remember
63 The Orphans' Kaddish: 1945
64 Let Your People...
68 The 20179th

These translations are dedicated to the memory of Suzannah Spira

András Mezei, Poetry and the Holocaust

AUSCHWITZ is a museum. The smoke has now dispersed, and each generation to the end of history must make peace with the past and resolve to live with our ability to attempt genocide.

András Mezei (1930-2008) has left behind a retrospective exploration of the Holocaust for our time. His voices of the past address us with an urgency and directness unheard within museum walls. There are many such voices speaking to us of terror, folly, greed, cruelty and absurdity. Mezei's poetry makes them sound like our own voices.

Mezei was a major Jewish-Hungarian poet. He survived the National Socialists' attempt at the 'ethnic cleansing' of Europe as a child in the Budapest Ghetto where some 17,000 souls perished around him from hunger, disease and the fancy of uniformed bandits.

Unlike other great poets of the Holocaust, like Paul Celan, Primo Levi and Miklós Radnóti, Mezei refused to come to terms with death. Indeed, his work is a celebration of the unconquerable spirit of his people. And unlike Anne Frank, he had the luxury of time to give voice to the concerns of the victims at the height of his literary powers.

I first met him shortly after the Second World War. We were both recovering from our experiences in the Hungarian Holocaust in a camp for Jewish children under the care of a Socialist-Zionist movement then called *Dror Habonim*. It was also preparing us for emigration to what was to become the state of Israel, mostly on board ships like the famous *Exodus* running the British blockade.

Mezei went. He found employment as a semi-skilled labourer, but returned to Hungary after a year and a half as he thought he stood a better chance of attracting a girlfriend there. Eventually he read literature in Hungary and became a poet, novelist and polemicist. Like many Holocaust survivors of his generation, he embraced enthusiastically the ideal of Communism in the hope of building a just society free of racial, religious and class prejudice. His first serious doubts arose over the brutal suppression of the 1956 Hungarian

Revolution against Soviet power.

Unusually for a Hungarian writer, his work has been published in several European languages (as well as Hebrew). He was a literary journalist most of his life.

After the collapse of Communist rule just two decades ago, Mezei founded *Belvárosi Kiadó* (*Budapest City Press*) and the *Central European Times*, the literary-political journal that forged a leading role in the debate and reconstruction of post-Soviet Hungary. He established a club that served as an informal meeting place for the writers, academics, politicians and businessmen. He used it to gain great influence in shaping Hungary's trade relations, specifically in the privatization of state assets and in the cultivation of commerce with other formerly Soviet-administered regions. Several high officials were appointed on his advice. He appeared oblivious to high-pitched criticism by his literary rivals behind his back that a poet ought not to soil his soul by the world of money and power.

I met him again early during the transition to democracy, when he commissioned me to translate his Holocaust poetry into English, I joined the editorial board of his journal and we became close friends. For me, our collaboration was part of a wider project, an anthology of the Hungarian Holocaust in English translation.

Mezei's father, a jobbing fiddler usually engaged in taverns and fairgrounds, perished at Auschwitz. Mezei's poetry draws on the culture of destitute, itinerant provincial Jews carving out a precarious existence in the rapidly industrializing, complex society of inter-war Hungary.

But the voices of the Holocaust speaking through Mezei's verse transcend the limits of class and nationality as well as the geographical frontiers of Nazi-occupied Europe. He called these pieces 'fact poems' as they are based mostly on his personal experiences, together with professional interviews with survivors, fragments of contemporary correspondence, medical and administrative records and analyses and post-war criminal proceedings.

Mezei, who won a beauty contest as a boy with golden curly locks, became short and fat in his old age with a shock of white hair beneath a wide-rimmed hat. I think he often deliberately acted out the anti-Semite's stereotype of the ghetto-Jew.

He was deeply religious, passionate and cantankerous, shrewd and naive, generous with his love and famously mean with his money. But he published a long list of worthwhile books at a perpetual commercial loss, unfailingly recouped from Jewish funding agencies, the post-Communist Hungarian political elite and the bewilderingly complex web of private enterprises that his heirs are now trying to untangle.

His experience of the war clearly shaped his life. The expression *Holocaust* (Greek for burnt offering) or *Shoah* (Hebrew for disaster) or *Pharrajimos* (Roma for dissolution) conveys very inadequately the impact of a nearly successful attempted annihilation of an entire culture.

The final and most destructive phase of the process began with the military occupation of Hungary by Hitler's Germany in March 1944, at a time when Allied victory in the Second World War was already obvious.

Less than three years earlier, an ultra-Nationalist government of Hungary – a minor, semi-feudal, East European backwater – had declared war on the incredulous governments of Great Britain, the USA and the Soviet Union in return for territorial concessions promised by Nazi Germany and at its neighbours' expense. Its ill-equipped armies were routed, its independence lost first to Germany and then to the Soviets.

Despite mounting repression and hysteria whipped up by the country's relentless setbacks on the battlefield, the largely assimilated Jewish-Hungarian population had lived in relative safety until the German invasion. The mass racist murder by industrial means of the Jews and Roma as well as the homosexual and the politically dissident minorities was introduced under direct German rule.

The ensuing Hungarian Holocaust culminated in the destruction of some half a million civilian lives (including perhaps 70% of the entire pre-war Jewish-Hungarian population and up to 50,000 Roma). The well integrated provincial Jewish populations and the other minorities singled out for annihilation were humiliated, robbed, massed into ghettos and other assembly points and transported in inhuman conditions to extermination camps such as Auschwitz-Birkenau in Poland and slave-camps such as Mauthausen-Gusen in Austria.

Due to diplomatic pressures, the deportations were formally halted before the capital could be completely emptied of the target populations. Tens of thousands of people there were crammed into specially designated tenements under armed control. Many others sought survival in hiding. Both groups were exposed to persecution by the law enforcement and paramilitary agencies, persistent aerial bombing by the Allies and the eventual three-month Soviet siege of Budapest whose ferocity is widely compared to that of Stalingrad.

In addition, tens of thousands of Jews were exposed to otherwise unnecessary perils of war, engaged in forced labour under Hungarian command or leased to Germany to work the copper mines of occupied Serbia. Hungary was the only power during the war to assign to the battlefield its own citizens – Jews – as slave labourers. Some 48,000 were deployed with the Hungarian invasion force to the Eastern front alone, clad in light civilian clothes in the bitter East European winter, to build fortifications on starvation rations. Many were casually murdered by their own commanders.

All this is little known to the Hungarian public, who were spared over the decades of the subsequent Soviet administration from the pain of confronting the country's shameful past. This explains the vulnerability of this region to neo-Nazi agitation at a time of economic insecurity. A new generation of historians is trying to change this. But Holocaust poetry remains an irritant in Hungary.

Some of the country's great Holocaust poets are largely ignored at home, although they are becoming known abroad. And those who cannot be ignored are often misrepresented. Generations of Hungarian school children have been required to recite Radnóti's poetry by heart, but they have been taught that he was writing about the general horrors of war rather than a specific genocide. They are still told that the poet had met a 'tragic death'-- not that it was racist murder committed with the approval or at least the connivance of the Hungarian majority.

Mezei started publishing Holocaust poetry only in

old age. So now do some others, albeit very cautiously. Apart from one brave and inadequate current attempt, I am not aware of a single anthology of Hungarian Holocaust poetry published in all the decades since the war. My own sources of original material are mostly small-circulation one-off collections, early Second World War publications, unpublished manuscripts and mass-circulation books whose contents are deliberately misinterpreted in lengthy analyses by literary/academic hacks.

I began translating poetry as a young man in the hope of learning from my betters. I saw myself as a fine-art student in a public gallery copying the work of a great master in order to learn his techniques by re-creating the same composition on a different canvass.

But there is now a very urgent, very different dimension. I believe that the poets of the Hungarian Holocaust like György Faludy, Ágnes Gergely, Éva Láng, Magda Székely, Ernő Szép and many others including András Mezei can now take their place in the European literary tradition. Their poetry may perhaps help the post-Holocaust generations – the descendants of the perpetrators, and of their victims, and of the passive bystanders – to face our dreadful joint inheritance together and learn to live in harmony.

Thomas Ország-Land, Budapest, 2009

Faces

Blessed be those whom I passed on the street,
those who beheld on my chest
the yellow Star of David,
those who were saddened by the sight,
those who walked on with heavy heart
burdened by shame; and blessed be also
those who chose to avert their faces
closed with fixed and frozen looks.

Flames

The ones who gave up their personal cyanide tablets
to spare a child from agony in the gas –
themselves have kindled the burning bush,

the ones who approached the end with dignity
herded to cruel death but not like cattle –
themselves have kindled the burning bush,

the ones who were able to dig their graves and toss
hell behind themselves with each clump of earth –
themselves have kindled the burning bush.

Blue Eyes

They who ravished the robust women
among my forbears, they our tormentors
still live within me to this day
with the spilled blood of our men-folk.

So many Franks and Slavs and Mongols,
brave blades of the pogroms, lurk in my bones
yet, by the right of the mothers, the Jew
stares back at them from my face.

They've changed my brown eyes into blue,
and made my curly dark hair blond,
that rabble of all Teutonic Europe
who gather and bustle and stir in my cells,

they who have dressed my bones in their skin,
their white skin soft like fancy linen –
But as the rabbis have blessed the fate
of the Jewish people in the offspring,

and brought them up, despite the rapes,
from age to age as Jewish children,
still the murderers have blue eyes
and blue eyed also are the victims.

Friday Evening

The table stands on pounded dirt-floor
covered by a white damask tablecloth,
with plaited milk-bread set out and prayer-books,
and some small candles already burning,
the silver candlesticks expecting
the moment when the Sabbath will enter,
the Bride will stand upon the rag-carpet
and join us in the empty chair,
the one by grandfather, and this night
no-one should be missing among us,
this pious family murmuring prayers,
blessing each piece of milk-bread in turn,
sitting together in the kitchen
where the fringes of the double-thick tablecloth
softly cascade down onto our laps,
I see fiddling fingers plaiting the fringes
for today is holy, holy, and
our hands today must do no work
as people who are joined by the Sabbath
must not even think of business –
I watch grandfather's Sabbath face
depart from time to time to Jerusalem
and return again when our eyes meet
as though his kingdom were right here,
and grandfather sits in peaceful silence
at the head of the great long table
laden for Friday evening with milk-bread,
laden with wine and candlelight,
he is the first to break and taste
the milk-loaf, to bless it and pass it on
to each of us for further blessing –

Every fallen crumb of that golden
braided milk-loaf collects here now,
the stars that have scattered from the timeless
table of God all gather here now,
but, my God, where is that Sabbath

the day when everyone could sleep longer
and grandmother read in the big double-bed
and my dangling feet did not reach the floor
and my eyes could not yet see past the walls
where a wagon was pulled up for us
with everyone brutally crammed inside...

Mother and I, the lucky survivors,
sit on one side of the great laden table:
the fringes of the double-thick tablecloth
dangle over empty space.

Voices

Suddenly I speak in my mother's voice.
Suddenly I speak in my father's voice.
Suddenly I hear my people speak
in my voice.

The Lists

They did not need quite 24 hours
in Győr, nor in Veszprém or Szombathely,
in all the small cities throughout the land
a register of Jewish residents
was assembled before the sunrise
the very day the Germans took over –
the lists were prepared in a sense of shame
and helplessness, in heartfelt regret,
you might say with the greatest of sympathy
and embarrassment. They were surrendered.

Poor Folk

If you and your family must be taken away,
at least do right by us, we are poor folk
and to you it is now all the same –
we'll send the children over to collect,
may the Eternal Lord keep you
and we will save your valuables,
in case you return.

Robbery, Naked

You won't be needing these, he said,
and flung my mother's photograph
among his booty, and my shirt.
I still retained heaped on my blanket
the things I had to bring: a mess-tin,
my boots and socks, warm underclothes,
a bar of shaving-soap – and I had
that irremovable mark on my finger
in the place of my looted wedding ring.

Memorandum

This lot possessed nothing. The lives of poor people
were cheap. A shot was cheaper than transport –
52 Gypsies, dealt with on the spot.

Letter from Nusi

And now at last we are quite certain
we shall be taken shortly – but where?
Kolozsvár? Várad? Újfalu?
And then the wagons? Where from there?
But you don't need to fret about us,
outside, the bags are all prepared,
the basket of food, a pot of honey,
a pair of backpacks, the bedding linen –
the cart is waiting by the portal
for grandma's ride (poor gran's old feet!)
and mum has sent a card to dad.
No time left. Still, what really matters,
the place is tidied up for winter.
Sanyikám, darling, I take my leave.
And tell our father he's in my heart.
Whatever our lot, we shall be safe –
God shall provide.

Derecske, 6 June 1944

Deportation

The people they've lived with in the village
are being herded in front of closed portals,
still and silent each. The fences
would conceal all sight, all feelings,
except for the tea-rose, the violet and weed
leaping through to reach out towards them.

The Roma

They could not read the deportation order.
They did not heed the thunder of the drums.
But they knew: immediately, they ran asunder.

Haste

After the Jews had been taken
the gendarmes combed through all of Derecske
and found granny Krammer in hiding,
she was ninety-three years of age,
and also Eve Németi's little brother,
just three years old and a day or two.
They were dispatched in earnest haste
to the rest of the transport still in Nagyvárad
to catch up with the deportation,
so that even those two should not be missing
from the round six million.

Deported Women

Deported women, still they are sitting
in that great timber granary
on their few precious, wretched objects
near Kőszeg, to this very day,

where my old mother defecated
as she sat there, and where the straw
stuck to my little sister's poor
urine-infected private parts,

and where my older sister sang
softly, eyes closed, hands on her ears
and squeezing her vagina tight –
still sitting in that great granary.

A Chorus of Pious Souls

A dreadful silence, even at Yom Kippur.
My Lord, there must have been a weighty reason.
The horror of the graves in mute fruition –
My Lord, there must have been a weighty reason
that no relief came in our desperation,
my Lord, there must have been a weighty reason:
instead, the gendarme came to us, death and oppression,
my Lord, there must have been a weighty reason,
the hell of Nagyvárad Ghetto, persecution –
My Lord, there must have been a weighty reason:
our words took wings, our souls... soared in devotion,
my Lord, there must have been a weighty reason
that He who had given the Torah showed no compassion
my Lord – there must have been a weighty reason.

A Choice

When the children were torn from their mothers,
and the ghetto was searched for tiny creatures
left in hiding, and the cries and the screams
were drowned by loudspeakers blaring out lullabies,
and the children were crammed into lorries, a German
soldier turned to one pleading mother,
> *How many children have you?*
> and she replied, *I have three –*
then he said, *You may take back one of them*
and helped her on board the vehicle
to choose one, as three pairs of eyes lit up
and three pairs of arms expectantly opened
towards her: *Mother, take me, me, me!*
...An eyewitness recalls that she
declined the choice. She left alone.
> *How many children have you?*
> She informs God: *I have three!*

Hiding

Inside, a baby crying. Outside, the search,
the trampling boots. The fugitives petrified.
Then someone hands a pillow to the mother.
The babe falls silent, silent. Silent!

Tumbrils

These two-wheeled tumbrils are not for milk-churns
nor for Tobias the milkman,
nor for the fruit
of the Indian summer,
ripe apricots, melons and apples on the canvas,
nor whistles, nor spinning-tops,
hairpins and bras,
nor labourers' shirts,
nor sewing-cottons, nor buttons nor boots.
These whining tumbrils
that bump along slowly
the desolate back-streets
carry no fleece-wool nor rags, nor goose feathers.
The peddlers do not sing.
Soft Kaddish and silence,
silence, silence,
lament behind them.

Roma Campsite

Clothing, canvas, rent and ransacked,
billow with the scent of death.
The needle nose of a woodland fox
patrols the damp, deserted campsite.

A Camp by the Village

I
That day, in the village inn at Balf,
the merrymaking camp commander
staked a litre of wine on the wager:
now, could he raise the courage to kill
a Jew, any Jew, right there on the spot?
And while he passed the time of day
over the wine, that day, in the camp,
no-one collapsed in the cold from exhaustion,
barefooted, shirt-sleeved in the snow,
while that litre of wine still lasted
the prisoners all survived that day, and
the calm of the Lord thus entered the camp.

II
Day after day, some people left open
the warm, dry carpenter-shop at night,
some did not bolt the stable door,
some heaped the coal on in the wash-house,
some requisitioned Jewish labourers
and let the weak, frost-bitten creatures
rest in the shed, some every day
left scraps of food in secret places,
some passed on messages and hope:
Ernest Wosinski, the manager
of the bath-house at Balf, and his family,
and John Fleck, the innkeeper at Balf,
and Margaret Jáger, and Lágler the baker,
and Rosie Pötl and Martin Pöltl,
and Mrs. István Szabó, a housewife.

III
There were ten just souls... But what crimes
weigh down the conscience of the village?
Had but the Lord seized only ten
scoundrels infecting the soul of the people,
Sodom would never have arisen
anywhere in this blessed country.

Statistics

No cry of anguish, no manner of wailing
is more heartrending than the sheer numbers:
147 trains
for the transportation in 51 days
of 434,000
provincial Jews by 200 SS troops
aided by 5,000 Hungarian
gendarmes and hundreds of volunteers –
they were detained at first in the ghettoes,
they were then taken into the brick-works
already stripped of their family savings,
then caged in cattle-trucks, 80 in each, and
conveyed without water and food to Mengele
from the first day of the occupation –
processed by people obeying orders
who never outdid the German commands
but willingly obliged the commanders –

Nearly half a million provincial Jews:
Nearly 10% of them stayed alive.

Delight

The New Hungarians, a patriotic paper,
called solemnly on 16th May '44
for the summary execution of 1,000 Jews
as retribution for each bombing raid on the capital.
Dad said, *Our patient newsprint can bear a lot.*
And after the following air raid, my father and I,
conscripted labourers marked with the Yellow Star,
returned elated from rubble clearing duty
and cheerfully carried our spades and pick-axes home
(an assembly point also marked with the Star of David)
for we thought the execution took place, so far,
only in *The New Hungarians*' columns.

His Own Command

He prescribed a frostbite ointment
for the sore foot of the guardsman.
And he still explained on the way
which chemist could supply it that day
under the rules of the early siege
of Budapest, as the soldier limped
along with him towards the place
of execution. The Jewish doctor
obeyed his own command.

Jason

She carefully unlaced her grandmother's boots,
then kicked off her own. Before the pair: the river.
Behind them: Jason, the neighbours' son from the square
lit by the frozen snow – and his machinegun.
Jason, discharging his first-ever magazine.
Jason, standing stunned as the tumbling bodies
are whisked away and gone with the turbulent current.
…Had he done that? Was there so little to life?

Gustav!

Feinstein, a Jew from Memel,
recognized his neighbour
in the execution squad.
And he cried out to him:
Gustav! aim
straight between the eyes!

Testimony

The people stripped off their garments.
They did not weep. They did not shout.
They did not beg for mercy.
A grey-haired woman standing by
the freshly dug hole in the ground
cuddled a baby in her arms – she
sang for it, tickled it, and the child
rejoiced in rings of laughter.

Psalm

I watch my spade as thrust by thrust
and spit by spit it shapes my home
till, like our psalms, my steaming breath
lifts rising from this cold, deep hole.
My Eternal God! Your very
being steels my arms. You know
that all the time till resurrection
will pass quickly like the thunder
of the gun.

Before My Fall

Before my fall,
before that great block of stone came tumbling upon me,
before it crushed in my chest,
before it rushed me into the land of shadows –
in the sight of the Lord
I had raised up all of Egypt.

The Masters

At Dubienka, the Germans mustered twenty
orthodox Jews. They marched them donning
their prayer shawls and phylactery thongs
and compelled them to recite their psalms
and raise their bare arms as they searched the sky.
Then they doused them with petrol and torched
their masterwork.

In the Bomb-Pit

His shovel clanged against the metal body
when he was forced to dig a funnel-shaped pit
around the unexploded bomb in the ground.
The explosives expert watched from a distance.
And, deep within his megatonnes of history,
the Jewish prisoner stood in the bomb-pit unharmed
as the expert cautiously descended
into that reality of war in which
Nebuchadnezzar's lions facing Daniel
must grow tame in the sight of the Lord
even within the steel cloaking of the bomb.

Tally

Counting heads at the gate,
the Düsseldorf guard kept tally.
Beneath a detailed statement
about the deportation,
1,007 lives
are described on the sheet
by groups of vertical lines
crossed out.

My Folk

Those tottering figures who wandered away
from the lengthy disintegrating
marching columns of the deported,
who left the highways
and took to the fields
soaked by the icy November showers
in flapping rags like windblown scarecrows,
those were my people, such easy targets
for the guard, folk hunted like rabbits,
yet who still attempted to beg,
yet who still were shot down while trying –
I remember them
every morning
when I take on the day and the dross
has not yet gathered in my heart.

Towards the Dniester

As the marchers dragged themselves forward,
the bare-footed peasants by the road
picked out the choicest boots and trousers
and, at their bidding, the guards
shot down the occasional well-clad prisoner
in exchange for a handful of notes.
The death-march stumbled on towards Orhei.
The peasants collected their wares.

Cattle-Trucks

It doesn't matter which wagon it was, and
whose lips held fast against that crack
between the planks of the cattle-truck,
who sucked clean air through that tiny space,
which district filled his lungs with the fragrance
of rain-soaked hay, of snow on the meadows,
it no longer matters who found that teat
in that crowded box-car amidst the putrid
steam of urine and stench of excrement,
who found it crawling among sore feet,
that nipple bursting through the crack
to feed him on oxygen-enriched air,
who feasted like a babe on the breast,
which prisoner's life was thus extended,
whether it was a Jew or a Serbian
whether a Russian or a Hungarian
whose heart at last could beat more calmly,
who has gained strength whilst surrounded by death –

and whose eyes have locked on to an unearthly crack
ever since then, in this blinded wagon
which is our world, that crack, that crack
admitting a light beyond our reality,
a light through which the whole train of cattle-trucks
passes forever with all the prisoners –
a light that burns like a beam from hell.

Possessions

Thirty-four cities throughout the Reich received
735 goods-trains comprising
a total of 29,000 wagons bringing
fabrics, carpets, paintings, sofas, bookshelves,
beds and dining tables, tablecloths, plates
and knives and forks and spoons and ivory chopsticks
and silver and imitation silver tableware
with a metallic taste… this loot collected
from 71,619
homes in Belgium, France and Holland alone,
possessions giving pleasure throughout the Reich –
if the final solution could not be otherwise,
at least the little bracelets, the evening shoes,
the fragrant ball-gowns by the baleful were welcome,
and the leather jackets and furs. The sender:
Dr. Rajakowitsch, Liquidation Dept., SS.

The Executioners

Still laughing, that Galician Jew's eyes, still bright
in the blaze of his beard set on fire by the killer's lighter,
eternally laughing, beyond even time and the final judgment,
and in his gaze thick heads of hair and earlocks and beards
set alight in a waxen white candelabra of bodies –

and the Almighty's face does not flinch in the flames.

Self-Portrait, Treblinka

I fire and I fire while retreating.
My mouth is belching blood, my eyes are smiling.
My strength is sapped, my weapon silent. I'm captured.
My mouth is belching blood. My eyes still smiling.

Christmas in Auschwitz

I
*Holding that child will cost your life,
young woman…* a slave of the camp warned Mary
on the ramp, before the selection. Today
that advice resounds a thousandfold.

II
When Mengele sent off Mary
and the Child towards the left,
the Saviour was even born
in the Carpenter's empty arms.

The Scale

Measured under Mengele's scale,
Peter stretched and strained but hardly
reached the string with the top of his head.
Béla failed and trod on regardless.
Tiny Árpi was led to the gas
still on tiptoes. The tallest among them
had to raise the string of death
over his head to get past the scale
and accompany the frightened
children, beneath the Eternal's gaze.

Group Portrait

The cows grazed in freedom beyond the deathcamp
and the air conveyed
their healthy munching
to the people promised a communal bath,
yet whose prayer was for gas: relief, at last,
in the bitter almond fragrance of Zyclon B2 –
in that passive state of animal existence
there stood (My God! hallowed be Thy Name)
a group of women
crammed together,
devoid of hair.

Hunger: Data

The skin turns bluish white.
The nails bend into claws.
The eyelids swell, and liquid
oozes from the tissues
beneath the skin and moistens
the swollen legs or hands
upon the lightest touch.
A coarse and wiry pelt
covers the body all over.
The eyelashes strangely lengthen
while, like a moth near the flame,
the victim slowly approaches
the ultimate transformation.

The skin turns deathly pale,
the arms, the legs, the torso
are bloated and the brain
becomes soft and dilated.
The heart has shrunk, already
it's smaller than its owner's fist.

The captive's daily diet
comprised 300 grams of soup
and 60 grams of bread.

If the Mother...

If the mother was taken from her daughter
to the gas chamber,
if the daughter was taken from the mother
to the gas chamber,
if the child survived,
if the mother survived,
if after Auschwitz the mother could still give birth,
if the girl-child could still grow into a mother
and re-create her parents in her offspring –
who would have endured more?

In their Place: A Daughter

My daddy's lost children: Eve and little Joe.
My mummy's lost children: Stevie and little Paul.
My daddy's marriage, a legendary love match.
But mummy mourned at every river – I know
she wished to die.

My daddy declared: his parents' graves lay here.
And mummy declared that people should not forsake
their parents' final resting place.
And thus they merged their equal losses, although
at first it was only
beneath the canopy,
for the law took its time to confirm
the death of mummy's husband and daddy's wife.

Mummy wanted no children
after Stevie and little Paul;
but after Eve and little Joe,
my daddy yearned for babies more and more.

That is why I am here. I was named
after daddy's late daughter. I live in their place.
My mourning father was 54 years of age
and my mother was 42
when I was born.

Exhumation

As most female corpses still
hide their features behind their shawls,

as their intertwined torsos and limbs
teach us about resurrection,

as one infant's small remains
reach to snuggle a woman's remains,

as that speechless jawbone still
nestles a baby's skull,

as the flesh decomposes, yet
these bones are bleached by the sunlight,

as that fallen mother's hand
recalls its endless, weightless chores –

thus the Eternal considers all
mass murders, each by each.

12 September 1945

Nightmares: The Survivor

How many nights must pass before
I need not wake up anymore?

The Street of the Dead

I walk along that street as though
nothing had occurred there,
I recall each face as though
the residents were still present,
I name the name of every soul,
from house to house I walk and call
my brothers who still live there,
together, beyond the present.

Blanche Schwarcz

Her elder son has emigrated
to Palestine. Her daughter Leah
has married in America.
But she, Blanche Schwarcz in the kitchen
with war-time lemon-tea substitute,
some goose-fat treasured in the pot
and brown bread on the table
(she is still busy day by day)
keeps spying through the curtain of
the years down to the dusky portal,
keeps glancing up to the square blue sky
framed by the ventilation shaft,
that small blind window on her final
residence in this world.
She stands outside by the well-wrung mop
that she has placed before her threshold,
she goes on rinsing the long red passageway
to welcome a new arrival.
She would never leave the ghetto
not till her younger son returns
...although she knows he will not.

I Remember

Like scorched grass, my bare life remains
after the pestilence, famine and terror –
The sword and fever have retreated:
I remember, I remember.

My beloved dead are moaning.
I've come from bottomless depths.
Skeletons on the towers of Babel:
I remember, I remember.

The sun shines even on the killers,
but still I shiver forever.
I soar with my gaunt and mighty angel:
I remember, I remember.

I stop the chase and suddenly turn and
wait to face my tormentors.
My chest is a gravemound, let them assault me:
I remember, I remember.

I have no city just one ruined gate
resounding inside and out with the endless
lamentation of poverty:
I remember, I remember.

Still alive, my eyes have beheld
wickedness beyond measure.
No longer do I need fantasies:
I remember, I remember.

Along the deserted autumn street
wanders a blind old beggar.
I defer to him from afar:
I remember, I remember.

The Orphans' Kaddish: 1945

The orphans saying Kaddish, praising Him,
after the genocide, praising Him the Eternal,
Kaddish said by the orphans, singing His praise,
praising Him the Eternal, after the genocide.

What kind of people are the survivors ready already to chant:
holy, holy, holy be His name, the smoke has not even
dispersed, the surviving people, chanting already, what kind of smoke
is this, not even dispersed, His name be holy, holy, holy.

His law will light up the broken eyes of the dead,
already it has lit up the gaze of the living,
the broken eyes of the dead lit up by His law
already, it has lit up the gaze of the living

praising Him, the orphans saying Kaddish,
the survivors, what kind of people are they ready already to chant,
the broken eyes of the dead by His law lit up:
holy, holy, holy be His name,
the smoke has not even dispersed.

Let Your People...

Let Your people perish, my Lord:
take pity upon Your own, I entreat You.
Let the basket of bulrushes sink.
Leave empty the tablets of stone.

Let the strings wither in the harps
hung high upon the willow tree.
Let longing song not lure them to suffering,
let them be swallowed by Babylon.

Let Your people die out, like the rest,
crushed down by the weight of other peoples,
let their lifeblood seep away –
Your restless people's restless blood.

Let Your people perish, to the last.
Take pity upon Your own, I entreat You.
As You have granted to other peoples:
let even their final seed be lost.

May the sea never part again.
May the heavens provide no manna.
May water not leap from the rocks
nor the guidance of law from above.

Let their blood flow with muddy waters.
Turn them into a plague of frogs.
Pull the survivors of Israel
deep beneath soft seething peatbogs.

Turn Your people into a hailstorm
ignorant of its mission and purpose.
Let it lay waste to its own dreams and
fail to pass through the Land of Goshen.

Turn Your people into darkness
rather than seat them in prominence
between the Almighty and the nations
marked for the role of the scapegoat.

For this people perceive the burning bush
even where human flesh is on fire:
have You accepted our hallelujahs,
my Lord, from the smokestacks of Auschwitz?

Do not stop the course of the sun,
like in Gibeon, but place the night
above Your people and bury Judah's
brilliant, mighty city of tents.

With the flame alight in the centre,
our sanctuary lamp thus burns through time:
like smoke from the oil-jar, our bitterness
inexhaustibly flows and rises.

You let six million burn in exchange
for only three lives in Babylon,
Shadrach, Meshach, Abednego:
those were your baits, whom You chose to rescue

unscathed in their coats and underclothes
from the fire that did not burn them –
but those three should have perished
deep in the flaming furnace

so that Your people might not have lived
ever since with the heat and stench of the fire,
so that Poland might not have become
the glowing throat of the furnace.

Empty. Empty. Empty. Empty.
In the impersonal silence of space
Your promises have flickered away
more intensely than miracles.

What did the world gain by Your driving
Your people into Nineveh
despite our stubborn inclination
drawing us on towards Tarshish?!

You have given us defeat and dispersal –
that alone should have been enough.
But You have also granted us yearning
for our ruined Jerusalem.

Had but the stone remained on the well
rather than that the wells of time
should tower above it: all those fleeting
too transparent, empty redemptions,

as Joseph led Egypt out of hunger...
Had but the stone remained on the well,
had but the man thrown into the well
remained alone in the bottom of the well.

You have granted us vision for solace
in the face of all torment – Had You
but smitten down Jacob with his ladder,
alone to the darkness of the stones...

Why did not Your pillar of fire
suddenly arise behind us? – Your people,
and Your word, would have expired
within it beneath your mountain.

You have granted us the scripture –
that alone should have been enough.
Had You but withheld the Sabbath
and given us just the bare firmament...

You have given us Jeremiah –
that alone should have been enough.
Had You but withheld the Lamentations,
Your stern and steep vast wall of stone...

Had You not granted us the Torah
in place of ruined Jerusalem,
its potent words instead of stones –
that alone should have been enough.

And You have given us Pontius Pilate –
that alone should have been enough.
Had You not also granted us Jesus,
and the forgiveness that never came...

Let Your people perish, my Lord:
take pity upon Your own, I entreat You.
Let the basket of bulrushes sink.
Leave empty the tablets of stone.

Let the strings wither in the harps
hung high upon the willow tree.
Let longing song not lure us to suffering,
let us be swallowed by Babylon.

Epilogue

Empty the wombs and keep them barren
Yourself, my Lord, if You can do that,
take back Your promise from Your people,
do not make our numbers mighty.

Jesus? – At times even a single
Jew is too much for a whole nation:
do not judge the peoples, my Lord,
according to the way they treat us.

And should You take pity upon us, my Lord,
which is Your prerogative,
lead with compassion the darkness of Egypt
out of Your cursed people.

The 20179th

Like ink on the blotting paper, the number
tattooed in Auschwitz splinters and spreads
on the inside of my lower left arm
when I ride the tram in the summer
and, forgetting myself, I happen
to reach up in my short-sleeved shirt
to hang on to the strap.

    * * * *

May I never lift my right arm
if I forget the mark on my left.

Notes

Thanks are due to the editors of the following publications where some of these translations have previously appeared: *Belvárosi* (Budapest), *Contemporary Review, The Forward* (New York), *The London Magazine, International PEN, Penniless Press, Pennine Platform* and *Snakeskin.*

Two collections of poetry by András Mezei are available in English - *Holocaust 1944-2004* (translated by Dániel Dányi, Thomas Ország-Land and Jon Tarnoc; Belvárosi Press, Budapest, 2004) and *Testimony* (translated by Thomas Ország-Land, Belvárosi, 1995). *The Miracle Worker*, a Holocaust novel (translated by Thomas Kabdebo; Belvárosi, 1999) is also available.

For more information about the experience of Hungarian Jewish and Roma peoples during the Second World War, see Imre Kertész, *Fateless* (Vintage, London, 2006), Alfred Pasternak, *Inhuman Research: Medical Experiments in German Concentration Camps* (Akadémiai Press, Budapest, 2006), Krisztián Ungváry, *Battle for Budapest: 100 Days in World War II* (I.B. Tauris, London 2003), Ernő Szép, *The Smell of Humans* (Central European University Press, Budapest, 1995), Monica Porter, *Deadly Carousel* (Quartet Books, London, 1990), Martin Gilbert, *The Holocaust* (Holt, Rinehart and Winston, New York, 1985), John Bierman, *Righteous Gentile* (Penguin Books, London, 1981) and Hilda Schiff (ed.), *Holocaust Poetry* (Fount Paperbacks, London, 1995).

The Yellow Star
Jews in the capital were compelled to display Stars of David on their chests and to live in the Central Ghetto or specially designated other tenements that were also prominently marked. These were located near strategic installations such as arms depots, bridges and railway junctions in the mistaken assumption that the presence of Jews would persuade the Allied bombers to avoid such targets. The separation and assembly of the Jewish population was also to facilitate its intended eventual mass removal to Auschwitz.

Burning Bush
A fire described by the Book of Exodus in the Bible, in which Moses perceived the presence of God.

Győr, Veszprém & Szombathely
Ancient cities in western Hungary with formerly large, prosperous Jewish populations murdered during the Holocaust.

Derecske
City in southern Hungary prospering by agricultural commodity trade. It lost its well integrated Jewish community and much of its Roma population during the Holocaust.

Kolozsvár, Várad/Nagyvárad & Újfalu
Kolozsvár (Cuj in Romanian) Várad/Nagyvárad (Ordaea) and Újfalu/Gyergóújfalu (Suseni), strategically seated Transylvanian population centres briefly under Hungarian administration during the Second World War when they were used as transit hubs for the deportation of people to Auschwitz.

Kőszeg
City north of Szombathely near the Austrian border used as an assembly point for Jews before their removal to Auschwitz.

Yom Kippur
The Day of Atonement, the most important Jewish religious celebration.

The Torah
The five Books of Moses comprising the basic tenets of Judaism.

Tobias/Tevye the Milkman
The hero of *Fiddler on the Roof* by the Yiddish master Sholem Aleichem.

Kaddish
A Jewish prayer for the dead.

Balf
An ancient spa near the Austrian border widely sought for its medicinal waters and rich bird life. During the war, it was the site of a slave labour camp where many inmates were worked, starved or beaten to death.

Sodom
A proverbial city of wickedness whose destruction by divine wrath is described in the Book of Genesis.

Mengele
Josef Mengele, physician and SS officer, stationed in Auschwitz for two years in charge of cruel and unscientific medical experiments conducted on live and initially conscious captives. He also supervised the selection of new arrivals for immediate murder or brief periods of intensive slave labour in the service of the gas chambers and crematoria and the processing of the possessions of the victims.

Memel
Prussian city, now part of Lithuania as Klaipeda.

Egypt
Mezei's references to the Biblical story of Joseph saving Egypt from hunger (told in the Book of Genesis) and the enslavement of his descendants by the Egyptians (Exodus) allude to the many services performed by Jews to the non-Jewish world and the persecution that they have periodically endured there.

Dubienka
City on the Polish-Ukraine border.

The Masters & The Executioners
These poems refer to some of the many photographs taken by the Nazis of themselves enjoying the humiliation and murder of their victims.

Daniel & the Lions
The Biblical tale of a Jewish hero in the court of Nebuchadnezzar in ancient Babylon subduing lions by invoking the power of God is told in the Book of Daniel.

Düsseldorf
German city, venue of the 1970 trial of Franz Stangl, commander of the Treblinka extermination camp in Poland.

Deathmarch
The notorious, often aimless march of large numbers of starved captives at a forced pace and under the blows of their armed escorts was a form of mass murder widely employed during the Holocaust.

The Dniester
River in Ukraine that empties into the Black Sea.

Orhei
Town in Moldova that lost a large Jewish population during the Second World War.

Possessions
SS Captain Erich Rajakowitsch of Trieste (part of the defunct Austro-Hungarian empire), a lawyer and trader, was in charge of the dreaded Section IV-B-4, Special Office for Jewish Affairs, in Holland, supervising the deportation of Jews and the appropriation of their assets.

Self-Portrait
The Treblinka extermination camp was destroyed towards the end of the war by an armed rebellion of its inmates.

Christmas in Auschwitz
In Jewish mythology, all human beings are the children of God. For Mezei, Mary is Miriam, a Jewess, Jesus (the Saviour) is her baby, Joseph (the Carpenter) is her husband.

Zyclon B2
This was the poison gas favoured by the Nazis for the mass extermination of people.

Basket of Bulrushes
A reference to the discovery of the infant Moses in the Nile described in the Book of Exodus.

Harps... upon the willow
A reference to Psalm No. 137.

Land of Goshen
An area of Egypt that Joseph's tribe had to cross to their appointed place of settlement as described in the Book of Genesis.

Gibeon
Ancient Canaanite city near Jerusalem conquered by Jewish invaders under Joshua's command.

Shadrach, Meshach and Abednego
Three heroes of the Book of Daniel that describes their survival through faith of an ordeal in a fiery furnace in the court of King Nebuchadnezzar.

Nineveh... Tarshish
Tarshish at the western edge of the Mediterranean was the intended destination of the Biblical figure of Jonah when he was diverted to the Assyrian capital of Nineveh beyond its eastern edge, as related in the Book of Jonah.

Stone... well
A reference to the betrayal of Joseph by his brothers.

Jacob's ladder
The dream of the patriarch Jacob of a ladder ascending to heaven is told by the Book of Genesis.

Pillar of fire
Divine guidance described in the Book of Exodus.

Lamentations
The Book of Lamentations.

Pontius Pilate
Roman governor of Judea, AD 26-36, responsible for the execution of Jesus.

The 20179th
Inmates chosen to serve as slave labourers in extermination camps were tattooed for easy identification.